Good Grief

poems & short stories

Good Grief

poems & short stories

Cale Maloney
Illustrations by Cass Cruz

DEDICATION

*To the God who created me,
the One who has never left me.*

ACKNOWLEDGMENTS

To my mom, who allowed me the space to feel. You never ostracized, but instead, nurtured and championed.
No matter what deck of cards was dealt to us, it was us against the world.
Thank you for never leaving my side.
This is for you.

ISBN: 979-8-9997438-1-7

I hope you're proud of me.

Rooms in the House

The First Time Grief Held My Hand

Maloney

Good Grief

Grief is a dear friend of mine.
His shoulder creates a perfect crevice for my fatigue to lay in.
He sits in the corner in the cold of the dark like a mirage of water in a desert, his colors are familiar and safe.
I become a radar to his presence. I can sense him like a storm in Alabama, my storm shelter is above ground.

The blanket of despair he provides is more comfortable than the embraces of the past—
at least his blanket doesn't come with knives to my back.
I light the candles, play the music, and lay on the couch when he arrives, as my bones begin to sink into the sea of anguish that numbs my ever-beating passion for optimism.
Like whispers in the air, a glorious symphony directs my dreams with an all-star cast. The film reel is one I've seen before, but the ending always surprises me — familiar, yet heart-shattering.

Grief has lasted longer than friendships, remained truer than my hopes and dreams, and shined brighter than my future, but remained colder than the hands of those who left.
Maybe we can call it good, grief.
Maybe we can call it good grief.

It's been a minute.

I hope you're okay.

Thank you for waiting for me.

your ghost called
my voicemail box is
full
maybe i'll
answer later
when I can
but again
it's full

it's so quiet, all
i can hear
is the sound of
my own
disappointment

in myself.

I have lost myself.

I'm not sure he's gonna
come back...

Good Grief

Soliloquies and solemn woes,
what hearts may break, time may restore.
What's left to love will be what's left to lose.
The race nears its end, but
they just keep moving the line.

Good Grief

i'm so tired
but my dreams
are just as
exhausting

i'm losing you

i'm losing you

i'm losing you

i'm losing me.

I want to apologize to myself...
I haven't met them yet.

I often don't see how absence makes the
heart grow fonder.
Separation just makes my heart tired.

some days I don't want to be mature,
I just want to be

okay

The Hurt That Was My Name

do you want me to change?

GOOD.

me too.

To me, a ghost story
and a love story are
the same thing...

Neither are real.

Good Grief

It's no longer a choice,
but rather, a TV show
through rose-colored
glasses that quickly
shatter and
diffuse.

Whether we'd like to admit it or not, fear can often know us more than we know ourselves.

We fear things like clowns, snakes, the dark, even... but fear can remind us of our failures, of who we are and who we are not.

Fear dances with us on the dance floor while whispering its minor key melody into our ears.

Who could we have been? Could they have been mine? Could she have been mine? Could I have been there for myself to have? What if they never left? Am I who I am, who I want to be, or who I fear? Who I despise? Who I loathe?

The two-way tango is just me and my shadow; I named him *Fear*. I hope someday we'll have our last dance... but I'd rather dance than recreate steps alone. I'd miss the synchronized footstep echoes proceeding mine.

Good Grief

A good workout increases strength. You can feel it in your legs, your core, your arms, your shoulders and your hands. It gets your blood pumping, the veins swollen–

/

You're doing great! Go until your hands match his. Until they match hers. Until they match theirs.

/

Feel the blood echoing in your system, each pulse, a name, each name, a new voice. The voices saying to become the wallpaper on the walls of your reality, silent and unmovable, strong, yet taken advantage of–

/

"What color?"
"White."

/

The hammers of betrayal break the walls, but you're still there — hearing all, seeing all. "I don't like that color if I had it my way, I'd make ~~it~~ him look real nice–"

/

cause that's what family does.

/

The way her hands became an unwelcome visitor to the party—~~opening~~ unraveling the bow on the present I wished to present to my wife, the way his hands built a tower around my throat–

/

Happy Birthday! Here's the gift, a reminder that you won't win.

/

The way their hands tinkered and fidgeted with my gadgets until they were too bored to play, a liability of my own melodrama that might have saved me.

did i break what was meant to be mended?
did i take what was meant to be given?
did the walls that became my defense come with blades of betrayal?
did i cross the line?

did i hold onto love when i should have let it go?
did i believe in a future that wasn't even mine to champion?
did the work of my hands become a labor of smoke and ash?
did i entertain you, but leave myself behind?

was it all painless, or did i just become numb?
was it all a mirage, or a dream i shattered?
was it left up to me, and i ran like a coward?
was my destiny a roadmap i threw in the trash?

did i?

I often think about the child I could've been...
I'm afraid to take on dragons and monsters of the deep. I could've been a translator for the world of the forest, speaking their language and embracing the undisturbed life.

Would I have been taller?
Stronger?
Braver?
Deeper?
Care-free?

Would the slabs of my foundation have been crafted on concrete? Would the trees have known me as their leader, rather than their weak prey?

Would the birds have been proud to sing their song to me, rather than roll their eyes as they sing their song of comfort to my broken spirit with nothing to give them in return?

Would the wolves have championed me on their team and welcomed me into their pack, rather than growl and sneer—

"You don't belong here!"

—while they morph into a kingdom I could never sink myself into?

Would the wind have lifted me to new heights, rather than whisper to the trees to sway a hedge of protection over me, keeping me in the undiscovered darkness, cold and quiet?

Would the king of the forest have taught me well and firm,

his eyes open with tears of joy as a bear does to its cubs, rather
than only show the shags on his back, full of thorns of
disapproval?
I could've been so much better.

I can be so much better than this, the grief I carry around in
my suitcase, decked with diamonds of insecurity and despair.
I can be so much better than the tidal waves of wrinkles that
splash on my face when the world goes quiet, and the voices
get too loud. I can be so much better than the growl in my
voice as it quivers its
melody of frustration and anguish. The song is called

"Why are you like this?"

It is sung by the choir that also stands in as the jury against
me in trial. I can be so much better than the shriveled eyes
reflecting the torments of the world in a reflection
painted in glass before it shatters and cuts my skin, the
painful shrieks spell out

"You are much worse than you thought."

I can be so much better than the hands that shake like a child
caught in a rain storm, holding clouds of tears,
unable to stay dry in the midst of a tsunami charging toward
them. I can be so much better than these legs, chiseled with
desolation, its crevices and small hills painting a journey of
smoke and mirrors leaving the hills of my legs to be as flat as
a desert I still can't make it through.

I can be so much better than this chest, a hollow and empty chamber of secrets that seems miles long, holding every snap of emotions, keeping the persona of the savior only to be a scam, a hoax, a weak and unexceptional experience hands will never embrace.
It holds a flicker of a candle that doesn't light up the darkness, but rather, tells it to have its way with it.

Good Grief

Remember and forget and remember and forget and remember and forget until I don't even know what I'm looking at anymore.

I watch you dance your dance with a ghost because at least that will last forever.

Give me space, give me space, so I can self-destruct and let you watch. Give me space, give me space, let me self-destruct and watch the splatter of the pain sprinkle the walls while you stand behind a clear shield of good moral points.

I don't seek pain, I seek revelation. Sorry they're synonymous.

Just let me decay.
Let me sink into my bed and it swallow me inside. Let my feelings turn off the light inside and allow the numbness to wrap its blanket of silence around me. Let my bones collapse under its white flag of grief, for they offer no weight of hope anymore. The brittle aches of self-reflection push a desire of reckless comparison that kills the light of joy, drowning the electrical cords in a sea that suffocates the me that I could've been, making sure they don't see the light either. A lose-lose battle with the overall win that maybe I can't change for the better...

I'm trying so hard to fit in with something that I made up in my own head.

They say "I can't lose you," but I've lost myself.

my heart is so tired of white-knuckling what
my mind tries to forget.
my heart is so tired of hearing the ringtone of
your laugh bounce across my eardrums, while
the dust of your ghost is all my hands can hold
onto.
my heart is so tired of laying on the soft place
to land, covered in roses, rooted in thorns.
my heart is so tired of being dehydrated, only
being washed with the acid showers that rain
from above, the desert of betrayal my eyes
roam.
my heart is so tired of the weight of the
invitation you forgot to mail, straining my
shoulders.
who knew paper cuts could be so inviting?
my heart is so tired of the dark, the absence of
my joy stripping the wallpaper off of the walls
with its passionate fiery love, my legs can't hold
the walls up anymore.
my heart is tired of the sound of its own rhythm
that no one seems to dance along to, the
orchestra is hitting its magnum opus, one more
measure is all it has before its final bow, the
mancando melody reaches its final note.

I gave you my promise,
but the game we both played had rules
of its own.

Don't cry for me,
your tears are acid in my sanctuary.
Let me do the honors,
at least mine will be safe to consume.

Maloney

The Lost & The Beloved

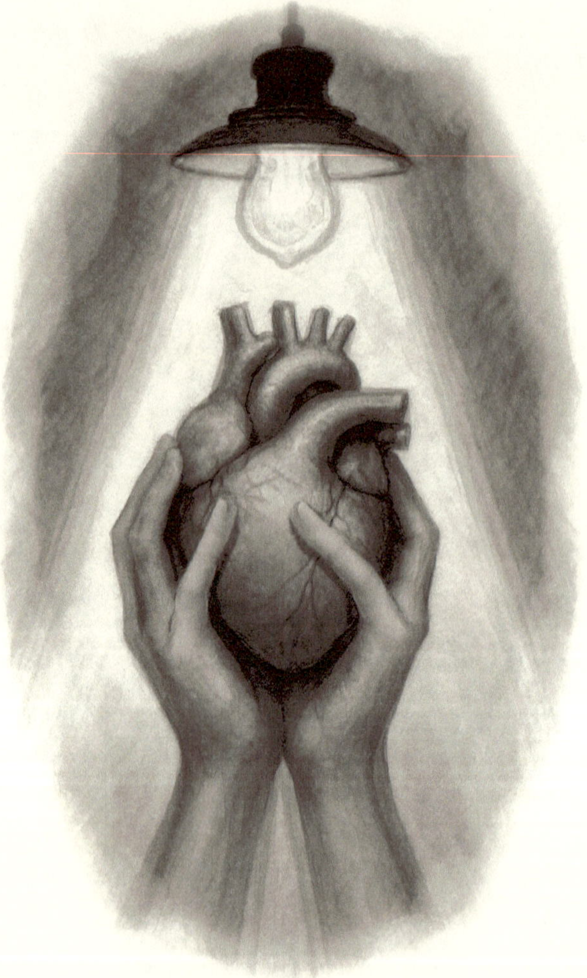

The bench is cold, the snow falling on her nose melts with each drop, blending in with the tears streaming down her face.

"You have to let me go."

The street lights yellow, the warmth shining on her face, like the day I first met her. Her freckles were constellations I'd recite night after night, like braille of my favorite story.

"You have to let me go."

My hands shake over my mouth, the island for her mouth that has become a desolate mission to mars, the valleys of each crease were the bar code that paid the price of longing I desired.

"I need you to do that for me."

But I can't... and I wish she couldn't either. The shadows speak, it's over.
Even if she was the starting pulse of my heartbeat echoes.

singing the song we used to claim as our battle cry, I pulled into the drive-thru of unforgiving memories. the melted asphalt singes the skin of my heart that forgot to wear a leather bond of protection around it, I know that was your favorite place to be.
the red dress
the red shoes
the red soul

the song that was the hook of the crochet, interwoven lines we'd read with our lips, piercing through time and space.

the chords laid out the timeline of our tragedy, the tombstone, our laughs, twinkles of inspiration we failed to post online. maybe we'd be hailed as the greatest love story if people actually read it.

the flasks of our defeats lined the shelves, each one engraved with the name of hope, the date of our shovels digging up the concrete of our forever home. the same signature that spelled "i love you" learned the new way to spell it, "i love this song".

Maloney

Good Grief

When I look at the sunset, I can't help but think
of the time I first met her.
She was wearing a red dress, soaked in roses, she
came up to me.
Her face carved my moon, and her freckles told
the story in braille that I couldn't keep my hands
off of.
When I see a red Cadillac, I think about the day
we got married, how we finally announced our
love written in the stars. The stars that night were
overwhelming, and I couldn't help but feel like I
caught the luckiest star in my arms that night.

Old and gray, I look in the mirror where she used
to stand, her hands still linger on my shaking
shoulders, her nails painted red like her dress
from the very first night I laid eyes on her.

The language of the pills spell out my
loneliness, and the red Cadillac across the
street just ended up in a junkyard, destined to
destruction and corrosion like my empty bones.

As I lay my head down, I get to see the sunset.
The one thing that is ageless in my life,
reminding me every day of your beauty, and while
I'm lonely, the warmth of that sunset still wraps
around me until I take my last breath.

My day hasn't come yet, but that doesn't
mean
yours has stopped.

What do I know about love?
Nothing.
Where does the love go when it runs out?
When does it leave?
Why does it die?
Do you kill it in one violent blow,
or is it a million unattended, unhealed little cuts and scratches?
What do I know about love?
Everything.
It creeps into my chest uninvited and untamable and I know love has no mercy on anyone,
Rich
Poor
Independent
Codependent
Confident
Insecure
It will bring you to your knees if you did it right.
What I know for sure about love is that you never come out of it the same.
The other person is a chemical
and I'm a chemical
and we'll both come out as different people than when we met.
I know when you're in love, kissing is everything, because words aren't the only way to tell a person how you feel.
I know when you fall in love, you feel like you're the first and only two people in the world.
Every kiss, every touch, every caress
is like something you feel that nobody has ever felt before,

and you think, "has everybody that's fallen in love before
just... walked around this nonchalantly the whole time?"
You're at a restaurant with your friends and you can feel it,
the secret under your tongue, burning like fire, but sweet.
And it creeps up to your cheeks and makes you smile.
And suddenly, you look down and see your heart's veins
reaching...reaching,
clinging to someone else's heart.
I've learned a lot about love in my twenties, but not enough
to maintain any control in the face of its power .
And for every new thing I've learned, there was something
else I couldn't understand.
All I know is, love changes you.
If you're lucky, to something better.
What I know for sure is falling in love with life itself makes
an artist out of everyone.
I thought I was making art before.
Taking photos was me making art.
But now I want my life to be the work of art, and my work to
be the camera that I take a
picture of it with.
It's what I'm living that's the art.
What do I know about love?
Maybe nothing...
And that's why it's everything.

the whispers of the past cry out
"what happened to us?"

the chipping away of the concrete of our history joins
"why did we change?"

let me mold together the vase of memories as I approach
our casket, let it hold the flowers of our innocence—
almost foreign.
the aroma is of a different tongue, I let my tears spread
watercolor mosaics on the sheets of our youth,
"did you leave me?"
or did I leave you?

please wish for me the bed of "letting go" I can sink myself
into, I wish you the best that life can provide—I am not
life, I am not the best.
forgive me, oh bones of dust, I hope you soar in the wind
over the flowers of your deathbed.
let me let go, go and let live.
i'll miss you.

Love is a painful religion. We worship at its altar of acceptance, we contort our limbs at its pleads. Cracking and shifting, our molds become fluid with no backbone for brace.

The rose-colored stained glass masquerade is the event of the year. Come one, come all—let's see if you are the last one standing in the dance of life, of sacrifice, of the religion of love.

The dresses are stitched, the makeup is primed, the instruments are tuned and the floor awaits. With each turn of the skirts, the flames are wavering. The challenge of the dance is to push the limit, to see how much of a muse can disappear.

The dance is simple: walk the tightrope in your heels, sing the songs of affirmation, and don't fall.

Don't fall. Don't fail. Don't die.

The tragic fabric of embrace is tested—left-step, right-step, don't step on each other's toes, or you'll break trust. Trust is an interesting thing—so hard to build, so easy to flee. Right-step, left-step, the rushed wind of colors matches the fleeting array of emotions—a Russian roulette of decisions, pick the right one.

One by one, they find their rhythm, you find your match. The flames attach, the protection is fought. The warmth is so inviting, its orange flow paints the sunset of each new day. I long to have the view never expire, it's as if I can touch the sun with my–

BURN.

An attack, a threat, an opposition, a fight. Destroy the flame, or let it destroy you. The flame keeps the music playing, you can't be left alone in the silence. You fight to keep the warmth, but the opposition no longer wishes for warmth, it wishes to flee.

When the candles blow out, the smoke fills the room—the scent of despair and agony become the statement piece in the walls. The wick begs to be re-lit, but the flame has become a ghost in the palace—the veil behind the masks, pleading for the buoy in the waters that never knows peace. The sound of the clocks echo the sounds of the footsteps of the past—maybe they've returned, or maybe someone new joins the celebration.

All that remains is the ash on the floor. The moment it's touched, it stains the face of the forgotten.

Paint a new sunset, wind up the sound machine, create the renaissance ceiling of love for all to see, but only for those to feel.

Amen.

the warm brown speckles of your freckles create a
constellation of honey I embrace,
a home as warm as the candle in the kitchen where we
danced with your blue hat, your red lips as red as my heart
when my soul aligns with yours, creating an ombré sunset
of your story I can stare at for the rest of my life.

the snow was pretty as it fell
but not as cold as the look you gave me
when i said i needed to leave.

the street lights were golden, just like your eyes were
the first day i met you,
and i can still remember what you told me.
"cat got your tongue?"

it's a strange reality to see after curiosity killed us.
the roof of our house was never completed.
i lost the hammer the day we played in the backyard,
but according to my broken bones, you found it.

i didn't want to leave you.
i never stopped loving you.
i just realized the only way you knew how to love me
was to hurt me.

I'm in love
with the moon.
She always sheds a light on me.
In my darkest moments
her crescents hold my tears
and her shadows keep my secrets,
even when it seems that I am alone.
The glow of her circumference can be seen
light years away, reminding me that
even in the darkest of nights,
I am not alone.

The Dust That Remains

Good Grief

The stoplight's red glow sheds a shadowbox of anguish, a cast of characters tell the story of the puppeteer's strings getting knotted and stretched, until the glisten of the blades finally halt the lifeline that supplied the cardboard shelter from the outside world.

I miss the comfort of your disapproval, the hug of your betrayal, the warmth of your absence. It gave me something to ponder about, something to look forward to, something to talk to God about. Your voice became the scratch on a mosquito bite, except I'm now covered in scars. Where's the band-aid?

The flowers have grown, but I'm the only one left to take care of them. Their aroma is laced with grief, but even the scent of grief can be good. It's a scent I can sleep to, a gas I can suffocate to. The dreams just replay the days, my favorites are the ones that won't happen. Apologies, apologies, and fears, and candles. Light the wick and bury me in my wooden coffin, at least there I can take a final breath, even with the dust of your fingertips working its way into my bloodstream.
It adds character, it makes you tough.

Down here I can grow with the seeds of the
flowers in my tear-shed garden. Away from the wind and the waves of the future, I can stay here, be my own grave-digger of the past.

Maybe I finally got it right.

The tears in this carpet can grow a garden.

He forgot love before he forgot the one he loved.
He watched as he began to seemingly devolve
backwards, while the world leapt ahead of him.

Her voice used to be the sound of home, now an analog
texture of audio on a recording machine, as
approachable as the newscaster on the nightly news.

To love is to forget, but to remember is to lose.
Each tick of the clock chips away at the walls of the
house built to house the symphonies of each major
chord, now speckled floor tiles cut the feet of those who
dare to trespass in the past.

I miss the old me. All of the old friends who used to care. All of the old, sad songs that just sounded sad but didn't increase the pain. All of the days that were filled with being careless. All of the fun times we would hang out. All of the texts that said, "I love you." All of the phone calls over stupid things we would laugh and cry over. All of the songs that were our theme songs. I miss the old us.

How does one feel so lonely in their own home?
The laughter turns into radio reflecting off the TV in
the room of heartbreak and destruction.

The sun commands the opening of my eyes,
and instantly I think about you.
The gas station where you always got your soda,
I remember your favorite order.
I wanted to keep you near.
I felt like I was losing my mind.

Each day began a cycle for optimism,
until the cold breeze of an unforgiving shoulder waltzed
in the room.
Little by little, each tone became a starling of relentless
distance I couldn't puncture the oceanic waves of.
Each laugh became a siren of isolation I became a
prisoner of.

What was once a doorway to living became the
crucifixion site of my death.
The soil I was buried beneath began to harden when the
tears ran dry. Sealed in my destiny of betrayal, I became
a patron of these arts, of this performance.

The body remembers what the mind tries to forget.
The moon commands the closing of my eyes,
and I suddenly begin to forget about you.

Maloney

Good Grief

Friendship is the burden that you wear around your neck like a necklace. "That's a cute necklace," they say at the party. The balloons, the confetti, the teardrops on champagne glasses—I hope they like me.

The chain is made up of expectations and promises you have yet to keep but will break. Sterling silver, just like the color of your face when you turn it from me, gray and cold—letting your silhouette be the movie poster I only have left to cling onto.

The jewels are rose, the color of the lenses that we both looked through as time washed away the sandcastle that we built; pirates and cowboys were our titles, the sky seemed so blue.

The clasp can hold the weight of despair, yet breaks at the sight of change. The mechanism clicks like the clicks of the buttons on our pictures, the bones of what had been corroded over time. The Polaroid picture becomes stained like my cheeks as it rains salty anguish upon them.

Wear it with pride, it's a daily battle you've chosen to win. Every battle must end, a knife to a gun fight, no boxing gloves allowed. May the victor's
necklace shine, though not too brightly, or it may catch the unsuspecting eye—the introduction of a new chapter that is already written by self-sabotage itself.

Dear you, the person I called my friend, my
"F-r-i-end...,"
I looked to you as best friend, only to be the dog thrown out onto the streets. When I asked for the light, I did not mean that you become the flame to my paper heart, the flicker of your words taking away my oxygen and leaving me to ashes. Your words sound as soothing as a rattle, and I, the baby, reached out to you, only to be bitten by your fangs. I repeatedly tell myself that we are just fine, but... are we?

Questions fill my head, determined to figure out what I did wrong, what I could've done better, what I could've done. Your name has become as sour as a glass of lemonade that I cannot sweeten, lemonade that I cannot swallow. Now I see why Beyoncé made her album, *Lemonade*. I called you my best friend, but you called me your "second-hand"—that second-hand that races around the clock as I stare into the mist of time fleeing from me, thinking about how you're determined to let me know how talentless, how pathetic, and how worthless I am. You have made it your mission to take each and every thing I find my joy in and shred it to pieces, leaving me with the rips and tears of my dreams.... I guess you can say you succeeded.
You s-u-c-c-e-e-d-e-d-d-d-dear...

You.
When I see your name in my head, it waves on a banner at the altar of the doorway. Yet, the terrace of my youth remained confined—off-limits. As a kid, I would cover my eyes when your bad side came out of the dark...the question is, why did I stop?

When you say, "I love you," all I hear coming from your mouth is "I am lying to you," and for some reason, I keep lying to myself about you.

I turn off my listening skills when you speak only because when I turn them on, I invite the daggers of your mouth in, slitting the wrists of my heart, and the blood of my passion seeps out on the floor, only to be stepped on by your rage-filled footsteps. The Holy Word says to turn the other cheek, but what if that one is bruised too? I dream of an ocean of peace between us, but how can I dip myself in that ocean when you are as dry as a desert? She says you are getting better, but what she really means is you are getting better at wearing your mask, a mask of deception that I can see right through. When I speak to you, my words feel as if though they are lifeless, leaving no impact on the change of direction of your train of thought, crashing into the front of that train and being left for dead, d-e-a-d-d-d-dear...

You.
You make the moon turn from a stranger into the only light I see in the hollow darkness. You slip under my covers at night and wrap yourself around my thoughts like a Band-Aid, a Band-Aid that, when ready to be ripped off, forms a glue that's as solid as my fake smile. You cover my mouth with your hand of discouragement, and if I dare scream, your screen plays back why I should keep my mouth shut. You have become a boom box in my head that I can't seem to pause, a voice that declares its desire of your acknowledgment, an ear-worm that I can't remove.

You guide me to the light, a light that shines even brighter than my friend in the sky. I feel that you are finally leaving me alone, only for you to drop me on the bathroom floor... this isn't the alone I had in mind. This isn't the alone I had in m-i-n-d-d-d-dear...

You.
When I see you in the reflection of that mirror, I see your red eyes, I see your dark bags, I see your quivering mouth. I see that all you want to do is scream your cry for help, but...you can't. You can't ruin that reputation you have outside of these four walls. You can't risk letting anyone know how you're *really* doing, even if that is your only saving grace left. You feel like you are on a period, but not like some sort of bodily period, but like an "all you want is for the world to stop spinning, your heart to stop racing, your head to stop throbbing, for him to stop hurting you, for them to stop betraying you, for your thoughts to stop..." period.

I remind you that tomorrow will be better, that tomorrow you will be able to live the happiest and the absolute best life that you've always dreamed about with real friends, with family, and real mental stability, but then... I wake up.

in a blanket of paper, tucked away in the book, lies
the forgotten memory of what could've been.
ink that has slowly decayed, showcasing colors that
perform an orchestral piece that only you can create.

she's glowing, a sort of medicine sweeter than honey.
her future was too bright, even for my own eyes.
she's sitting in a chair, a soft place to land after a
day of the world claiming her as their battle-fought
prize. she always felt alone, but couldn't hear her own
thoughts over her field of fans, like cicadas lusting
after her approval.

he's sitting on the couch across from her, cold and
liquid delusion in his hand, a smile that is held up by
puppeteer strings, eyes that are afraid to rest, ears
that hear the crowds of disapproval without a footstep
to trace. to be held would be to die, but maybe death
isn't as much of a shock as living has become for him.

the polaroid sat in that book, and while the world left
them battered and bruised, the photograph
remained untouched, unchanged, untormented.

maybe someday they'll know peace,
if only they could laminate themselves in that
memory left behind.

Maloney

I can hear it—
the laughter glistening in the sunlight,
the texture of the forgotten memory,
the invitation to dream and change the world that surrounded me.

His eyes, button and plastic, yet the keepers of my darkest secrets.
His ribbon, emerald green, a staple piece that hung on the door each time I'd knock.

Stitches surrounded him, my tears healed them. His skin, a map of each and every offense cast my way, like arrows let free from a quiver, a force field from the pain that would strike.

Knobs on his head perked up each time I called his name, now covered in dust with a full voicemail box —I haven't hit play in so long.

To forget is to relinquish, but to disobey the obligation of preservation, I'm sorry for becoming the thing that kept me up at night with acid rain upon my face, upon your head.

At least it gave us something to bond over.
Until we meet again,
I had the time of my life with you.

wooden crests traced the floors
dust danced in the sunlight
the creaking of the walls recites the incantation
of the shadow's summoning
I remember the way I felt when I first walked in.

summer of '04, the paint was new
the sun was a hug
the chairs could hold the weight of my
shoulder's world
the TV could still play those home movies I wish
stayed reality.

the toaster was the only thing that smelled like it
was burning
now the flames of the dark have left the remains
of hope on the floor, ash to be swept away in the
wind of forget.

I miss that place sometimes. I go to it when the
current world begins to become too
unpredictable. At least back then, the sun set at
the right time.

they call me the grave-digger,
the man who takes his shovel of despair
and uproots the laces of the past.
the skeletons are carved with regrets and anguish
they trigger me, but I'm the one who shot the gun.
each year, the grass grows taller, the flowers bloom
brighter, and the sand becomes more cleansed, but the
grave remains.

I walk through the terrain, my boots strapped with
repetitions of assurance, the boots carved with aged
leather, stained with the liquid life I took under my
wings.

I just don't understand the addiction of breaking the soil
of the beloved that crumbles in my fingers, the
rain-soaked aroma of the wind's efforts to solidify the
casket of the past smack my face like they did when
above the soil.

why do I keep coming back?

someone once said "old habits die screaming," but I
don't hear screaming... instead, I hear invitations of
betrayal,
and I guess I accept.

Good Grief

Where the Sun Still Sets

Maloney

Let the wind flow through your hands.
Let the oxygen fill your lungs.
Let the moon be your best friend.
Let the tears slowly drip down your face.
Don't wipe.

Consider the car horns, and let the melody of the streets
become your highway.
A plunge, a revelation, the submersion of the colors
waltzing hand and hand with the sounds as the bass knocks
on the door of your imagination.
The world is dark, the pit of your
stomach.
The tracing over and over until the muscles sing in memory
of the past.

Allow the rush to choke reality, and
allow the masquerade of your sight to project shadows in the
light, inviting the lovers and hard-feelers to dance in the
boom-boom-boom of the night.

The blankets, a sea of both safety and fleeting despair muffle
the rhythm of the heart, laying on the chest,
reaching for the sun.

The liability of making you stay.
Maybe the blanket isn't foreign, maybe this world isn't
empty. Maybe the key is the fingerprint of the breath from a
gasp, the spark of a collage of feelings.
Memories.
Memories.

Good Grief

Feelings breathing in and out, turning open the door to the
world that you make it.
Understand that the Louvre has art,
painting the walls with connections and invisible strings.
Look up, notice the clouds, they drift.
Drift.
Becoming the canvas to your paintbrush,
the invitation of the broken and depth.

I used to lock the door, but now in my home I live freely, the
lover of my mind in the taxi cab I am alone, but I am free,
and you can be too.

the sunset is my favorite color.
the clarity of a blue sky, the freshness of a stormy sky, the openness of a night sky, those are great.
but, a sunset is a color
a multitude of colors
a chorus of strings and harmonies and symphonies that rejoice that you made it to that special point of the day.
an invitation to watch the film reel of your life with grace, and patience, and acceptance.
maybe sunsets are made, not to alert you of an ending, but remind you of a new beginning.

come with me
let's ride off into the edge of what is known
where defeating dragons and saving the girl is
everyday activity, and the peasants proclaim,
"*hail the one who has succeeded!*"

let the clouds float in the bright blue sky, and
flagpoles become the precipice we land on, unafraid
of the ground below us, but afraid of not living to the
fullest.

the winds and the oceans are the percussion, and the
sunsets are the strings, creating a field of dilution for
the mind, a place lacking muse, a call to the
victorious for wearing the white flag of surrender,
at least here we don't have to fight.

The sunset starts to catch on fire, alarming the world that the day is coming to an end.
The cold stroke of a tear creates a path embarking on its journey, down the side of my tired and worn face.

As the sky paints its kaleidoscope fanfare, I hear nature's silence as it understands that all things must come to an end. My old and broken bones align with my soul, a house that creeks its loneliness, an Alcott without a voice, fighting its last fight, I cannot win.

As a lay, preparing my body for its final hug, my skin broken as an old blanket affected by all seasons, it loosens its white knuckled grip, a cry that is too tired to be produced, gasps no more. The soundtrack of memories hits play, I can hear the joys and heartbreaks of the life I was held in, not captive, but in a holding cell.

I open my brittle and cracked mouth, the lips shaped the banner of the final cry, "I can't go any longer..." The sunset embraces the tired effort and exclaims, "Here's the paint! Here's the brush! Now, paint your epilogue. It's needing a home."

One final breath seals the frame, it is now displayed for all.

I often wonder how the sun feels.
Some admire it, some despise it, some critique it, some hide away from it, some talk to it, some just listen to it.

Every day, it has to fight to make sure the depression of being wanted, and then unwanted, and then wanted over and over again doesn't seep into its rays. It watches everything. People live, people die. People win, people lose. It's idolized, and rejected.

All it wants to do is provide safety, warmth, healing, peace.
In return? Nothing.
No hugs of gratitude, no "good job," no ribbons or stickers, no celebrations of joy or laughter... but when it goes into hiding, they exclaim its purpose.

The sun is confident, the sun is strong.
The sun finds joy, rest, purpose.

I wish to be like the sun.

deep calling after deep
what hearts can't bear, your shoulders hold
reach out to me in my despair
hold me tight, see my grief, see my sorrow

may your love wrap me up in a blanket
a shelter
a home
creating waves of rhythms, heartbeats aligning

seek me and find me
may my tears sing the songs i can't form
may my trembling test the endurance of your steadfast
encounters
don't leave me here alone

these scars and broken dreams cry out
but your presence whispers under the noise
my flesh drowns in the ocean
but the waters still say your name

even when others have left, you stayed
what my hands have forgotten, your soul reminds
may you never give up on me

Good Grief

thank you

ABOUT THE AUTHOR

Cale Maloney was raised in the church, and was surrounded by the creative world of theatre since being a young child. Seeing the world through a creative and emotional lens, Cale drew near to God through creative measures in times of loneliness, grief, and even euphoria. Poetry became an outlet from frustrations, but ended up becoming a lighthouse of exploration as he entered a local poetry slam, solidifying his passion for poetry and creative expression.

After giving his creativity a home, Cale now seeks to use his creativity to impact people in a way that God impacted his own life.

ABOUT THE ILLUSTRATOR

Cass Cruz's early years were shaped by faith—though her relationship with God deepened after becoming a parent in 2020. A lifelong creative, she found her passion for drawing early on and continues to refine her skills through art and graphic design classes. Now focused on digital illustration, Cass loves bringing ideas to life through expressive character designs.

Her art often helps others tell their own stories—whether through spiritual tattoos, memorial portraits, or meaningful logos. For this collection, Cass' illustrations reflect themes of grief, nostalgia, and healing, echoing the book's message that beauty can grow from pain.

www.ingramcontent.com/pod-product-compliance
Lightning Source LLC
Chambersburg PA
CBHW020419150626
46554CB00014B/2028
* 9 7 9 8 9 9 9 7 4 3 8 1 7 *